ABORIGINAL
HEALING ORACLE

MEL BROWN

ROCKPOOL

Rockpool Publishing
PO Box 252
Summer Hill NSW 2130

rockpoolpublishing.com
Follow us! **f** **◉** rockpoolpublishing
Tag your images with #rockpoolpublishing

ISBN 978-1-925682-36-6
Copyright text and artwork © Mel Brown, 2018
Copyright design © Rockpool Publishing, 2018

Edited by Lisa Macken
Designed by Jessica Le, Marcella Cheng,
Rockpool Publishing
Typeset by Typeskill

Printed and bound in China
10 9 8 7 6 5 4

CONTENTS

Aboriginal ancestral wisdom - future

INTRODUCTION

We would like to acknowledge the land on which these oracles are being used, and wish to humbly pay our respects to the Ancestors of the past and thank them for their courage and resilience, which they have passed on to us during their journey on this earth.

We want to respectfully acknowledge the Australian Elders and Aboriginal Peoples of today, as we have the responsibility to shape our future and be role models in our strength and wisdom for our younger generations.

To our future generations who have yet to begin their journey or to even walk on their country, we eagerly look forward to the future you will create and the pride you will bring to us.

And to our other brothers and sisters, we ask for your respect and understanding while we walk our journey and continue to be the proud Australian Aboriginal People that we are.

In my Dreaming, the Ancestors share knowledge and wisdom in the hope it is used wisely to effect better outcomes for those who are open to listening to what they have to share.

Our Ancestors have lived lives prior to our existence and can see the future before us. It is within this knowledge that the Ancestors take the opportunity to shed light on the darkness that sometimes envelops our soul and leaves us questioning the future.

This oracle set is given to us as a tool to give meaning and understanding to the past, assist us to identify strategies to move forward in the present, and finally complete your reading with meaningful words of wisdom to illuminate your future Dreaming.

HOW TO USE
THE CARDS

· · · · · · · · · · · · · · ·

Aboriginal Healing Oracle has been created to enable
the reader to undertake a traditional three-card read
of past, present and future whilst encompassing
Aboriginal healing within a holistic approach.

Aboriginal Healing Oracle comprises three separate
decks of cards, with one each to represent past,
present and future:

Aboriginal bush medicine deck (past)
Aboriginal animal totem deck (present)
Aboriginal ancestral wisdom deck (future)

Each individual deck draws from ancient Aboriginal
knowledge of bush medicine, totem animals and
ancestral wisdom to provide readers with further
understanding on the clarification they seek.

Shuffle each of the three decks separately and at
random, then:

1. Choose a card from the Aboriginal bush medicine deck. The cards in this deck will reveal how the past is affecting your current situation. It may also reveal what is blocking or helping you move forward in the situation. The information revealed here can help you learn from your past.

2. Choose a card from the Aboriginal animal totem deck. The cards in this deck represent the events that are currently taking place in your life, and suggest possible strategies and outcomes relating to this situation.

3. Choose a card from the Aboriginal ancestral wisdom deck. This deck represents the outcome of the situation and provides affirmations from the Ancestors to encourage you and give you confidence to move forward and change the present.

DADIRRI

. . . .

*The word, concept and spiritual practice that is dadirri
is from the Ngan'gikurunggurr and Ngen'giwumirri
languages of the Aboriginal peoples of the Daly River
region (Northern Territory, Australia).*

*Permission for its use has been granted by
Ngan'gikurunggurr Elder Miriam-Rose Ungunmerr.*

A special quality, a unique gift of the Aboriginal
people, is inner deep listening and quiet still
awareness. Dadirri recognises the deep spring
that is inside us. It is something like what you
call contemplation.

The contemplative way of Dadirri spreads over
our whole life. It renews us and brings us peace. It
makes us feel whole again. In our Aboriginal way we
learnt to listen from our earliest times. We could not
live good and useful lives unless we listened.

We are not threatened by silence; we are
completely at home in it. Our Aboriginal way has
taught us to be still and wait. We do not try to hurry
things up. We let them follow their natural course –
like the seasons.

We watch the moon in each of its phases. We wait for the rain to fill our rivers and water the thirsty earth. When twilight comes we prepare for the night. At dawn we rise with the sun. We watch the bush foods and wait for them to open before we gather them. We wait for our young people as they grow; stage by stage, through their initiation ceremonies.

When a relation dies we wait for a long time with the sorrow. We own our grief and allow it to heal slowly. We wait for the right time for our ceremonies and meetings. The right people must be present. Careful preparations must be made. We don't mind waiting because we want things to be done with care. Sometimes many hours will be spent on painting the body before an important ceremony.

We don't worry. We know that in time and in the spirit of Dadirri (that deep listening and quite stillness) the way will be made clear.

We are like the tree standing in the middle of a bushfire sweeping through the timber. The leaves are scorched and the tough bark is scarred and burnt, but inside the tree the sap is still flowing and under the ground the roots are still strong. Like that tree we have endured the flames and we still have the power to be reborn.

Our people are used to the struggle and the

long waiting. We still wait for the white people
to understand us better. We ourselves have spent
many years learning about the white man's ways; we
have learnt to speak the white man's language; we
have listened to what he had to say. This learning
and listening should go both ways. We would like
people to take time and listen to us. We are hoping
people will come closer. We keep on longing for the
things that we have always hoped for: respect and
understanding.

We know that our white brothers and sisters
carry their own particular burdens.

We believe that if they let us come to them,
if they open up their minds and hearts to us, we may
lighten their burdens. There is a struggle for us, but
we have not lost our spirit of Dadirri.

There are deep springs within each of us. Within
this deep spring, which is the very spirit, is a sound.
The sound of Deep calling to Deep. The time for
rebirth is now. If our culture is alive and strong and
respected it will grow. It will not die and our spirit
will not die. I believe the spirit of Dadirri that we
have to offer will blossom and grow, not just within
ourselves but in all.

Aboriginal bush medicine

PAST

1. AUSTRAL BUGLE

Cleansing, release, calming

Austral bugle medicine allows you to see how things can be without the influence of others.

The opinion of others is 'their' truth and not necessarily yours. Opinions are formed through an individual's judgement and experience, and each person's view will vary depending on the way in which the experience affected them.

If those around you experience things differently and your views contrast with theirs, then the ability

to stand strong within your own truth becomes a challenging task to undertake. Often it is during these times that our determination is challenged, and the strength of our conviction is weakened.

Upon reflection …

The optimist in you refused to be affected by those with negative views, yet these very views made you doubt yourself … but don't! You interpreted the situation exactly how it was.

BLACKWOOD
FLEXIBILITY

2. BLACKWOOD

Flexibility, clarity, advancing

Blackwood medicine encourages flexibility in thinking, to clearly understand those with differing points of view.

Being open to other's beliefs is an admirable trait, as it demonstrates your ability to acknowledge the importance of allowing others to share their stories with you.

To understand the stories of others is a humbling and beautiful trait to possess. When

people are drawn to those who they believe truly understand them they will open their heart and share their stories, knowing the listener is sharing their journey.

However, this understanding can also become a double-edged sword. The challenge is when the listener becomes part of the story and also embarks on the journey. Sometimes too many journeys can take their toll, both physically and emotionally.

Upon reflection …

On this occasion you suddenly became everyone's confidant, yet inadvertently you shouldered the responsibility of ensuring the mob remained peaceful – but this came at a cost.

3. BRACKEN FERN

Reactive, painful, irritation

Bracken fern medicine is so irritating that it has manifested into physical pain.

Ignoring the issue does not mean they are resolved; it simply means you must deal with them later. Sometimes waiting till later can be a benefit, provided the intent is to devise a way to manage the situation more effectively.

However, when you're just ignoring the situation hoping it will go away, often it simply intensifies

the problem and makes it worse than it was in the beginning. Time tends to distort the truth and taints things in a way that changes the original truth of the situation.

While we can discount our feelings and mute our voices, the body has other ways to express its emotional pain. Before long we find ourselves being inflicted with physical illness, which has manifested because of ignoring the real issue.

Upon reflection …

At least you got sympathy for a physical illness, but being sick only added to your burden and frustrations. Rather than making good decisions, you found yourself in a worse position.

4. CHERRY BALLART

Courage, optimism, hope

Cherry ballart medicine brings courage and hope to those who are optimistic.

Positivity is not always welcomed by others, particularly if they themselves are hurting. For some the sheer sense of hope only highlights the fact they are in despair and further exasperates the situation, adding to their feelings of hopelessness.

When you express your hopefulness, others may be too scared to feel the same way. While enthusiasm

can be contagious, it can sometimes be destructive –
particularly for those who are not in the same
position and are fearful of being hurt even more
if the promises of 'sunshine and rainbows' don't
come to fruition.

Upon reflection …

Optimism from others was gravely lacking. The
hope you tried to generate only increased the fear in
others and highlighted the fact that the situation had
become unmanageable. The small amount of control
they possessed was better than none.

CHICKWEED
GROWTH

5. CHICKWEED

Expansion, growth, increase

Chickweed medicine encourages you to develop
and grow.

Growing does not occur without change, yet
change can sometimes be unimaginable. For some,
the power of knowing what to expect and how to
control it provides them with a sense of security,
which has become a survival technique.

Be wary of interfering with survival techniques,
unless there are other skills with which to replace

these with. What is taken away must be replaced, or else cracks begin to open up and holes begin to form. Sometimes, however, the cracks simply fill with water and provide the opportunity for new growth to begin.

Upon reflection …

Growing is sometimes downright scary, but when you were pushed – yelling and screaming the entire way – you landed in a far better place from which you began. Once you got your bearings, you were presented with an opportunity that was worth the traumatic experience.

6. FARMER'S FRIEND

Shifting, questioning, perception

Farmer's friend medicine allows us to see through the exaggerated views of others.

The views of others are merely their perception and are considered their reality of the situation. Our previous experiences – both positive and negative – inform our views and shape our belief systems.

Different perceptions of the same experience can lead us to questioning ourselves because we may see things differently. This does not mean either view is right or wrong, just that there are variations of the same theme.

When we experience things that touch on past unresolved emotions, then our reactions can become exaggerated. It is empowering to understand where these emotions might be coming from to better understand how they are affecting ourselves and those around us.

Upon reflection …

You wanted to ask questions to seek clarification but resisted, knowing at a deeper level the situation is not as dire as it seems. This was a hard decision to make, as it meant you had to trust your instincts and then justify why you delayed in making a decision. But you were right to take your time, weren't you!

7. KANGAROO PLUM

Truth, honesty, cleansing

Kangaroo plum medicine is connected to truth and honesty.

Speaking one's own truth is a rare thing that takes courage and trust, not only for the speaker but also for the listener. However, there is a responsibility to speak your truth in a way that does not hurt or harm others. Hiding behind the words

'I have a right to speak my truth' does not mean it gives you the right to hurt others.

Our honesty can sometimes hurt or heal. Speaking your truth comes with a responsibility of bearing the consequences of how your truth impacts on others. Equally, it is important to accept that others have their truth as well, which may not be the same as yours.

Upon reflection …

Being the seeker of truth, you have been somewhat surprised at the honesty afforded to you. So much so, you did not believe the truth when it was given to you – but it was the truth.

8. NATIVE GERANIUM

Releasing, calms, pacifies

Native geranium medicine accelerates the healing process.

Within any healing process there are many factors that determine how quickly we heal. Our healing process will be determined by our will and ability to embrace our new life in a way that is different from the time when the hurt occurred.

Progress can be scary and takes courage, as this often means experiencing pain. You are the driver on your road to recovery, therefore you have control over the route you take and the time it takes and if you will be distracted by diversions along your journey. Any road trip is a good road trip, provided you get to the final destination intact.

Upon reflection …

When we heal more quickly than others, it can leave us with a sense of guilt for being able to move on while others remained stuck in their trauma. There was no shame in looking forward to the future, provided you had respect for those who needed more time to heal and you didn't flaunt your 'I found the light!' attitude when others were still in the midst of their healing process.

9. OLD MAN WEED

Opens, expands, clear sight

Old man weed medicine makes it difficult for you to breath.

Breathing: it happens without thought and is part of the many functions our body undertakes for us to live every moment of our lives … until something occurs, and you realise that just breathing is an effort.

Stress and trauma affect the way in which we breathe; it affects our very sense of survival. Until

we regain control of the life force that is our breath, our lives and our ability to function are put on hold. Everything that happens outside of our survival mode becomes unimportant.

Upon reflection …

When all your efforts have been put into merely surviving, you didn't have time to hear. You were clearly told what the situation was, but you were so distracted you missed the importance of what was being said. Think back carefully and you will remember being told.

10. SPINY-HEADED MAT-RUSH

Refresh, rehydrate, rebirth

Spiny-headed mat-rush medicine allows you to understand and better comprehend the complexity of the situation.

Sometimes we make things so difficult that to manage the situation becomes insurmountable. Often this is an excuse for us not to undertake the challenging work and search for the answers that might require us to change our behaviour or beliefs.

Change is not easy and means leaving old ways behind to adopt new ways. Changing our ways can bring with it opportunity or just simply healing, but whatever the change is, know that it brings you closer to your recovery.

Upon reflection …

The past situation kept you stuck in that moment of time, reliving the trauma to such a point that it was emotionally debilitating. Your fear of facing the future was unwarranted and is the reason you are holding yourself back.

When you face your fears, you will quickly realise how much precious time you have wasted fearing the future. The way ahead is bright and wonderful – you need only put your fear aside and claim this future that is awaiting you.

11. TEA TREE

Energy, stronger, content

Tea tree medicine allows you to heal from your wounds, both physical and emotional.

Rejuvenation takes energy; energy makes you stronger; strength gives you a sense of contentment. Recognising contentment is often elusive, because we are already moving on to the next big thing before appreciating what we have already accomplished.

Being able to achieve a sense of serenity can be arduous work but is worth the time you spend seeking it, because once you recognise contentment and experience it you finally understand what it is you are missing in life.

Upon reflection …

You were tired and running on empty, yet you did not take the time offered to rest and re-evaluate. Your need for total control and the energy it has required to maintain this domination robbed you of your chance to become stronger.

Healing is an exhausting yet necessary task to undertake if you wish to move beyond this situation. Let someone else take control for a while and give yourself the time to heal; then you can come back even stronger.

12. WILD FENNEL

Calming, relieving, gentle

Wild fennel medicine is gentle and calming.

Finding the happy medium between doing nothing and responding in a forceful manner is a skill that takes extensive practise to master. Often doing nothing at all and leaving it to the Ancestors to manage may seem like the easiest option, but ask yourself first: are you using this as an excuse to avoid the situation?

In most cases, managing situations with a calm and gentle planned approach will provide us with the best outcomes, even when those around us are responding on a totally different energy level.

Upon reflection …

Your situation required a slow and measured intervention to ensure a positive outcome, however, you confused this situation by doing nothing at all. Doing nothing caused the situation to deteriorate beyond your control. Being laid back or passing the responsibility to others has not been helpful. It required a gentle response to relieve the situation.

Aboriginal
animal totems

PRESENT

BOGONG MOTH
SAFETY

13. BOGONG MOTH

Safety, freedom, courage

The Bogong Moth is a nocturnal creature who feels most safe at night when others are resting. During the dark, Bogong moves freely without fear of being seen, and in daylight hours finds shelter in dark places to wait out the busyness of the day. To some degree Bogong is a chameleon, blending into the surroundings to witness yet not be seen.

Part of Bogong's survival skills are the large spots on each of his wings that resemble large eyes, warding off predators by tricking them into believing Bogong is bigger than he actually is.

The artful way in which the Bogong bluffs and the bravado that keeps him safe in an environment where he could easily be overpowered by larger creatures are further testament to his ability to adapt himself to fit comfortably within many different situations.

Current situation …

It is time to stand up and be seen: no more hiding in the background and allowing the world to pass you by. You are fearful of predators, yet there is no actual danger to you – just your own fears.

You see things others miss, simply because they are caught up in the busyness of their own lives, whereas you can sit in the dark and take in what is happening, making perfect sense of it all.

When you voice your opinion others will listen, as you have a presence that people find calming, encouraging trust in you. So, step up and have your say.

14. DINGO

Shy, belonging, trusted

The Dingo is our shy desert warrior who prowls his land in search of where he belongs or who he belongs with.

Alone or in a pack, Dingo is fiercely independent and confidently fends for himself. Should he choose to live as part of a family, he will share the responsibility of ensuring younger ones are protected and cared for.

Dingo has the ability to turn his head 180 degrees in both directions, so nothing ever escapes

his attention. While he possesses an inquisitive nature, Dingo will watch from a distance rather than join; he is often mistrusting of others.

Current situation …

Just because others are not joining in does not mean they have something to hide or shouldn't be trusted. Understand that they have had negative experiences in the past that have hurt them deeply, therefore they feel safest at a distance.

Allow them the space to be a fringe dweller while this situation unfolds, but be aware that should they make advances to join the group they should be treated respectfully and sensitively. Most importantly, allow them to join without everyone making a fuss; if you do make a fuss, they will retreat again and probably won't return.

15. ECHIDNA

Steady, focus, protection

The Echidna waddles at a slow pace yet is determined to reach his destination, never distracted or straying from his purpose. If obstacles appear on his route he simply improvises, changes direction and goes around them, never losing sight of the purpose of his journey.

Echidna's ability to carry on regardless of what is happening around him demonstrates his skills to keep focused and attain his goal on completing the task.

Echidna knows danger is always present, and even with the protection of his quills his underbelly is soft and is not protected by his bristly exterior. Should he experience any threats along his way, Echidna will simply dig himself into the ground to protect his belly and will patiently wait for the danger to pass. When it is safe, he resumes the journey on which he began.

Current situation …

Things are moving slowly for you, and you have a worrying sense of fear in the pit of your belly and it feels uncomfortable. You have developed a healthy respect for your intuition, and right now your senses are tingling and you need to take note of it.

Your usual response is to make quick decisions and move on; however, in this instance moving too quickly and making rash decisions will not alleviate the fear. Perhaps you should consider 'digging in' and waiting for the situation to pass.

This situation doesn't really call for an immediate decision to be made and, in waiting a while for things to settle, you will experience an entirely different outcome – a pleasant one at that!

16. EMU

Curious, energetic, opportunities

The Emu is the most inquisitive of creatures, with a curious nature to explore his surroundings, in the hope of finding other interesting things. Emu is the eternal optimist, always searching for situations that he can turn into opportunities.

Possessing the gift of curiosity and a boldness that provides him with the courage to take chances and go places he has yet to explore, Emu is not afraid to seek out further knowledge.

Emu is an impressive teacher, role modelling his

inquisitive behaviour to his young chicks. His young quickly learn that seeking new experiences is not to be feared but embraced as part of their nature; his chicks will learn that the journey itself is part of the knowledge they will gain. And, in Emu's own travels, he will open himself to boundless opportunities.

Current situation …

It's time to look further abroad for what you need to truly fulfil you. While you are not unhappy with your current circumstances, there is a nagging curiosity you can't seem to shake.

Over time your curious nature has given way to being conservative, which leaves you feeling bored with life. Remember as a child how your curiosity took you on many adventures, even if the adventures were only in your imagination? Seek some of that childlike energy and resist the fear that has stopped you from taking advantage of new opportunities.

Others will notice your bravery and follow suit. Before long a new wave of people close to you will be trying new things, all because they saw the difference it made for you. These new opportunities that are opening up to you are life changing.

17. Frill-necked Lizard

Brave, strength, invisible

The Frill-necked Lizard is a desert dweller. While Frilly is small, he becomes a formidable presence when threatened.

Left alone, Frilly will blend with his environment and carry out his business without anyone noticing he is there; but threaten him, and this meek little creature will double his size by standing up on his back legs, raising his frills and menacing his adversary with wildly snapping jaws.

It's all a bluff: when Frilly knows he may not win the battle, he turns tail and runs away at breakneck speed on his hind legs to hide under a rock or up a tree till he decides it is safe again.

Current situation …

Not all battles need to be fought and not all battles will go in your favour.

Your honesty is getting in the way here, so try a little bluffing. Puff up your chest, put on the big stern voice and speak up – really speak up.

While this is a war you may not win, you will win a few skirmishes in the process of the battle. More importantly, you will emerge with a newly gained respect from others, simply because you stood tall and strong and didn't back down until it was necessary.

You will instinctively know when it's time to back down, but this is not defeat, this is just a truce until you regroup and regain your strength to battle again.

KANGAROO
INTUITION

18. KANGAROO

Intuitive, nurture, protective

The Kangaroo is a very intuitive animal and is always aware of what is happening in its environment. During times of drought when food is scarce, female Kangaroos do not have babies. This is a way of ensuring the survival of its young as they will not starve.

Female Kangaroo does not see her young a burden as they grow and continue to rely on her long after their time for independence has arrived. She takes her parenting responsibilities seriously and

will fight anyone who threatens her young.

She is the ultimate mother, never shrinking from the burden of her obligations, even when the time has long past for those who she is responsible for can easily fend for themselves.

Current situation …

Ask yourself who you are taking on the burden of responsibility for when they can well look after themselves. Somewhere along the way you have forgotten why this has even happened. It's like you're on autopilot and haven't taken notice of what you're doing for some time.

Those around you can see the burden you are carrying yet are too worried about saying anything, as you are fiercely committed to continuing on as is.

It's time to finally let go and leave the situation to manage itself. You have done an excellent job getting this far but you now need to allow the situation to run its course, otherwise those who you are protecting will never be able to grow and move forward from this situation.

19. KOOKABURRA

Friendly, fun, respect

The Kookaburra is a friendly bird, always happy and full of fun and laughter. While Kookaburra likes living with his family, he also appreciates his independence. Somehow, he finds a balance between them both.

Kookaburra is well known and respected for the ruckus he creates when others invade his territory, and will fiercely defend his home from others who come uninvited.

Kookaburra is also known for his talents for watching over his environment and will shriek loudly

48

to alert everyone when there is danger lurking in the undergrowth. This behaviour provides others with the opportunity to escape to safety before the threat becomes serious.

When Kookaburra makes his presence known, others stop and listen to his well-respected and trusted voice.

Current situation …

Know when to make a fuss or when to let things go. You usually avoid any types of confrontation and have become skilled at it, living what looks like a quiet and peaceful existence. The flip side is that you are often being left with the feeling you should have done more. In this case consider sharing your concerns with others, because your concerns are real!

Others are too caught up in the 'smoke and mirrors' and have no idea what is happening. When you share your knowledge and voice your concerns, it has the potential to make a significant difference in the direction this situation is heading. Although you're uncomfortable in speaking out, take big deep breaths and do what needs to be done.

20. PELICAN

Social, security, growing

The Pelican is a very social bird who possesses a strong sense of family. They are committed to their relationships and enter into partnerships for life. Outside of their families they are more vulnerable and do not thrive well in solitary life, therefore they seek the security of partnerships at an early age.

Pelican can often live in large colonies where together they work to ensure all family members are cared for. They intuitively understand the significance of relationships to their survival.

While Pelican is commonly known to inhabit coastal areas, they are very adaptable and can be found anywhere there is a source of water. Pelican will move to more appropriate surroundings rather than stay somewhere where their family will not thrive.

Current situation …

Family provides you with a sense of identity that is very important to you, however, you need to recognise the strengths of people you are not related to by birth. These can include friends, neighbours and work colleagues who are equally important to you.

Look beyond your family for support in this situation, as they won't understand what you're experiencing right now. It is wonderful to have a protective family, but sometimes the very protection they offer is what smothers you and prevents you from growing.

You need the support of others who are close, as they see you differently to how your family sees you and are unaffected by your family expectations.

PLATYPUS
PRIVACY

21. PLATYPUS

Private, elusive, harmless

The Platypus is a unique creature unlike any other animal in the world. On the surface Platypus resembles a combination of a duck, a beaver and an otter, but when time is taken to really see him Platypus is something quite different.

Platypus is elusive and is not often seen in his natural habitat, unless you should accidently stumble upon him. Platypus makes his home in burrows deep within the river bank and raises his babies in the safety of his home.

As cuddly as these creatures seem, they have venom-producing spurs that can be lethal to other animals and excruciatingly painful to humans. Their looks can easily deceive others into believing they are harmless and non-threatening, but get too close and you will bear the consequences.

Current situation …

Keep a low profile right now. Don't be the topic of conversation, as others are feeling scared and threatened and will clutch at anything to justify how they are feeling.

The others don't understand the situation and see it differently to what it actually is. People are very emotional and are overreacting to this situation in a way that you cannot understand. The situation is not that bad, but everyone thinks it is!

They have no other way to deal with their emotions than to place the blame on someone else and make them responsible; at least in their eyes, someone will be held accountable. They are actively seeking a scapegoat – don't let it be you!

POSSUM
STRATEGY

22. POSSUM

Invisible, strategic, unafraid

The Possum spends his day sleeping where he cannot be seen yet is in plain sight. An observer needs to spend time really looking for this elusive creature and is often surprised to find Possum right under their nose.

When day becomes night, shy Possum transforms to a sociable creature who bravely explores his environment in search of opportunities. Possum is unafraid of the night and takes chances that he wouldn't take during the day, simply because

he feels safe in the dark and has strategies to manage night-time dangers.

Possum's ability to move freely in the branches of trees and competently navigate the dangers on the ground is testament to his agility. His ability to adapt to whatever situation arises is his key to survival.

Current situation …

Don't wait any longer to show people who you really are. Hiding in the shadows is a safe place to hang out, but you miss out on so much. You have the same skills as everyone else, but don't like the attention.

You want to join in but are uncertain about how others will accept you. They have been respectful and allowed you your solitude, but will be welcoming of you if you choose to come forward.

It's time to find the balance between the shadows and the light and become part of the group. Be assured you will be fine – you may be a little uncomfortable at first, but within a short time you will be wondering why you kept yourself hidden for so long.

23. TAWNY FROGMOUTH

Merge, consideration, risky

The Tawny Frogmouth is the master of camouflage, and his ability to blend and sit quietly observing his surroundings provides him with the opportunity to see things that others miss.

Being the master of illusion, Tawny Frogmouth will adapt his pose to either blend with a tree trunk or pose as a broken tree branch, all the while knowing he is hiding in plain sight. He possesses the ability to evaluate situations while remaining at a safe distance, but keeps all this information to

himself. He is an expert at secrecy.

Tawny Frogmouth does not share his knowledge and insights, as this will expose him and make him unsafe. There is strength in keeping secrets and respecting that others have a right to manage their business as they see fit.

Current situation …

Sometimes watching from a distance allows you to evaluate things from a unique perspective and provides you with an insight that you wouldn't ordinarily have been able to gain. Witnessing the 'bigger picture' allows you the opportunity of understanding issues from other perspectives and viewpoints.

While you may be feeling you have been excluded from decision making, fear not; it has given you an insight that you would not have gained if you were right in the middle of things.

After more careful consideration, you can go ahead and make your decision and know it's the right one.

24. WOMBAT

Solitary, challenge, awkward

The Wombat is a solitary creature who prefers his own company rather than that of others. His singular focus of meeting only his own needs can be confused with selfishness, when it is merely his skill in minding his own business.

Wombat appears to dawdle through life at a slow and steady pace, not concerned with what is going on around him; however, when the situation calls for a quick and hasty response, Wombat possesses

amazing agility and speed that surprises those who expected him to be slow and clumsy.

Wombat builds his home deep underground in a burrow, complete with sleeping chambers. Interestingly, his home is always built with at least two exits, thus enabling him to escape should he be ambushed by opportunists. He can rise to any challenge and not only protect himself, but will fiercely defend his own territory.

Current situation …

Sitting in the background and running away from a situation does not mean you will not be affected by what is happening.

Eventually you will be forced to make decisions and choose sides. Rather than being surprised by this development, be prepared to act rather than react. Gather your information and prepare now, not later, because the delay may restrict your options.

In this situation you need to ensure you have a range of options available so the decisions made are best for you, rather than what others think is best for you.

Take control, but ensure you have an exit plan in place.

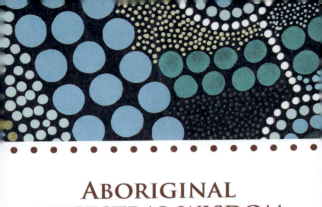

Aboriginal
ancestral wisdom

FUTURE

25. ALINTA

Acceptance, fearless, unique

'Indifference is the ability to allow others to have their own experiences without fear of judgement.'

Trusting in the future …

The Ancestors know it is a skilful art to accept people's differences without being judgemental. To allow other people to walk their own journey without fear of judgement is a divine gift, as it allows them to walk and live in their own truth and be who they truly are.

Aboriginal Dreaming totem

Each of us was born into our lives to have our own individual and particular experiences, no two lives ever being the same. We need to trust that our past, present and future are not random and they should be honoured as part of the unique journey that we embark on during our time on this earth.

26. KIRA

Attentiveness, breathe, insight

'If you quiet your mind, you then hear the message you're receiving.'

Trusting in the future …

Be still and listen to the messages which are being whispered to you by the Ancestors. The Ancestors are generous in sharing their knowledge, but you need to be still to hear the quiet whispers in which they speak.

Aboriginal Dreaming totem

Breathe. Heal your tired body and allow your spirit to find its peace. Within the quietness of your mind your body can begin its journey of healing, which in turn will replenish your weary soul.

27. ELLIN

Compassion, kindness, gratification

*'Kind-heartedness is the true
essence of compassion.'*

Trusting in the future …

Being kind to others is a truly selfless act that is
repaid by the Ancestors in many ways. In a world
were self-gratification is widely practised, kindness
is less often manifested yet is more rewarding than
one could imagine.

Aboriginal Dreaming totem

*There is often no acknowledgement of acts of kindness, yet the
very feeling you get when you are kind to another is powerful
and is rewarding within itself. The kindness bestowed on
others is as equally rewarding for ourselves.*

28. BRINDABELLA

Contentment, serenity, contemplate

'Contentment is appreciating that place within where serenity and happiness can be found.'

Trusting in the future …

The Ancestors want only for you to be happy and to find that place within us all where we connect to pure happiness and peaceful serenity. Upon finding such a place, nothing is impossible for one to achieve.

Aboriginal Dreaming totem

Breathe. Feel the sense of contentment within your being and contemplate its meaning. It's a feeling we find difficult to put into words, but true contentment does not require words; it just requires appreciation.

29. MIA

Faith, instinctual, expectations

'Trusting in your own instincts is the biggest leap of faith you can make.'

Trusting in the future …

The Ancestors do not subscribe to blind faith, as it can be misrepresented as trusting others before you trust yourself. Search your heart for what feels right and makes sense for you. If you have enough faith to trust in your own instincts, then the journey ahead will exceed your expectations.

Aboriginal Dreaming totem

Open your heart and seek answers from the finer details that get lost in everyday translation. It is from within that the answers to your questions can be found; however, having faith in these answers is where the real trust begins.

30. ALLORA

Forgiveness, worthy, peace

'The hardest act of forgiveness is the act of forgiving oneself.'

Trusting in the future …

The act of forgiveness is a deed of generosity that is often difficult to afford to those who have hurt us. Those who can free the darkness of an unforgiving spirit are rewarded with a sense that only a peaceful heart can experience.

Aboriginal Dreaming totem

True forgiveness is a challenging act to undertake, as it means having the ability to understand the humanness of ourselves. The words of forgiveness are only worthwhile when they are demonstrated with the kindness of forgiving yourself.

31. LENAH

Gratitude, ego, self-love

'Being grateful is the art of appreciation of yourself and then extending this gift to others.'

Trusting in the future …

Self-love can often be confused with ego, yet the Ancestors want you to be loving towards yourself. If you cannot freely love yourself, then what you have to offer others in return is insignificant. The Ancestors encourage you to love others, as they themselves love you.

Aboriginal Dreaming totem

Loving yourself is the most important act we ever undertake. It is difficult to do which is why many of us struggle, yet those of us who find true love for ourselves experience a deep and powerful sense of 'self' and need not look to others to understand and accept who we truly are.

32. JEDDAH

Honesty, love, pure

'In your search for honesty, first look within.'

Trusting in the future …

Knowing your own truth and trusting in yourself to be true to your beliefs is one of the greatest acts of love you can bestow on yourself. The Ancestors express love in its purest form and want you to love yourself in the same way.

Aboriginal Dreaming totem

Being honest in what we believe is a difficult challenge, but one that is worth the effort it takes. We may not all have the same beliefs; however, if we demonstrate humility in the way in which we share our beliefs we will gain respect from those with whom we are sharing our stories.

33. JANALLI

Integrity, honour, reliability

'First, honour yourself, then others will follow suit.'

Trusting in the future …

Finding respect and integrity in yourself will make you the person other people strive to be. The Ancestors want you to be your very best, so become the role model everyone looks up to. The start of this process is honouring yourself.

Aboriginal Dreaming totem

The truest way to honour the gift of life we were given is to become the best we can be. Our interactions on this earth provide us with the opportunity to embrace our humanness and learn from our experiences. By honouring ourselves, we then open ourselves to the wonderful journeys this life has to offer.

34. INALA

Loyalty, belief, sacred

'Trust and devotion are gifts that should be earned and not given because of the instructions of others.'

Trusting in the future …

Loyalty is earned as a result of your actions and beliefs and cannot be demanded of another. The Ancestors know that loyalty is hard earned and can take considerable time to gain, but once gained that devotion will be long lasting and sacred.

Aboriginal Dreaming totem

Loyalty means the total acceptance of another soul. Loyalty towards others should be used sparingly; however, loyalty to yourself is a true mark of self-respect. Know yourself first and trust your inner self to guide you to others who are worthy of your loyalty.

35. ALKIRA

Selflessness, sacrificing, future

'Self-sacrificing is only honourable when your sacrifice does not impact on yourself.'

Trusting in the future …

Self-sacrificing is an act where you selflessly give or act in a particular way towards another. The Ancestors warn us that being a martyr is not self-sacrificing, as often the choices that are made do not impact others, only yourself.

Aboriginal Dreaming totem

Give to others only after you have cared for yourself. The act of giving can only be worthwhile if we provide it from a place within us that has something to offer. Once we determine what we actually have to share, our gift becomes more valuable to the person we are sharing ourselves with.

LOWANA
WISDOM

36. LOWANA

Wisdom, listen, trust

'Trust your own wisdom before that of others.'

Trusting in the future …

Ancestral wisdom is born of those who have passed before us and are open to sharing their knowledge. This transfer of knowledge can only be attained if you spend time in conversation with the Ancestors. Stop and listen and benefit from the wisdom that is available to be shared with you.

Aboriginal Dreaming totem

Ancient knowledge comes to us in many different forms, gained from a single random thought or feeling. However, to the contrary, none of this is by chance. The challenge is within ourselves to trust the messages that are shared with us and then act upon them accordingly.

ABOUT THE AUTHOR AND ILLUSTRATOR

• • • • • • • • • • • • • •

Mel Brown is an Australian Aboriginal Ngunnawal woman. She both writes and illustrates her card decks, and her work is inspired by the deep connection between Mel's Australian Aboriginal spirituality and her relationship with the country in which she walks and with the Ancestors that she shares her life with.

Aboriginal Healing Oracle has developed from Mel's work as a consultant to Aboriginal communities and the government of Australia. Mel has an understanding that the need for healing is a way to reclaim spirit across all cultures.

ACKNOWLEDGEMENTS

· · · · · · · · · · · · · · · ·

Aboriginal Healing Oracle is a gift from my Aboriginal Ancestors that is channelled from the universal wisdom from past Caretakers of this land. I am continually humbled by the trust they extend to me, which enables me to share their wisdom with others.

I wish to acknowledge the wisdom of our Aboriginal Elders past, and the courage of our Elders present. Together both past and present Elders guide us with insight and teach us resilience to allow us to grow through each generation in a truly meaningful way.

I humbly thank you.